THIS BOOK BELONGS TO:

_____

YOUR NAME HERE

_____

OR HERE. WHATEVER. IT'S YOUR BOOK.

THIS LITTLE PIGGY WENT TO MARKET

in the City

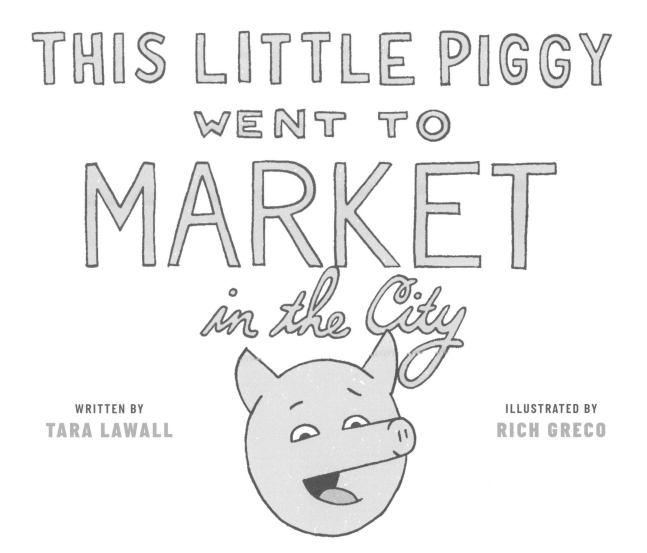

WRITTEN BY
TARA LAWALL

ILLUSTRATED BY
RICH GRECO

A MODERN FARM-TO-TABLE PARODY

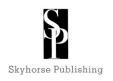

Skyhorse Publishing

To Cora and Rhett, my kids.
The best and worst
things I've done to my life.

—TARA LAWALL

To Ella and Eoin,
my child and
my child, respectively.

—RICH GRECO

This little piggy went to

MARKET IN THE CITY.

I'M GOING TO THE MARKET.
OKAY.
SLOP LOCAL

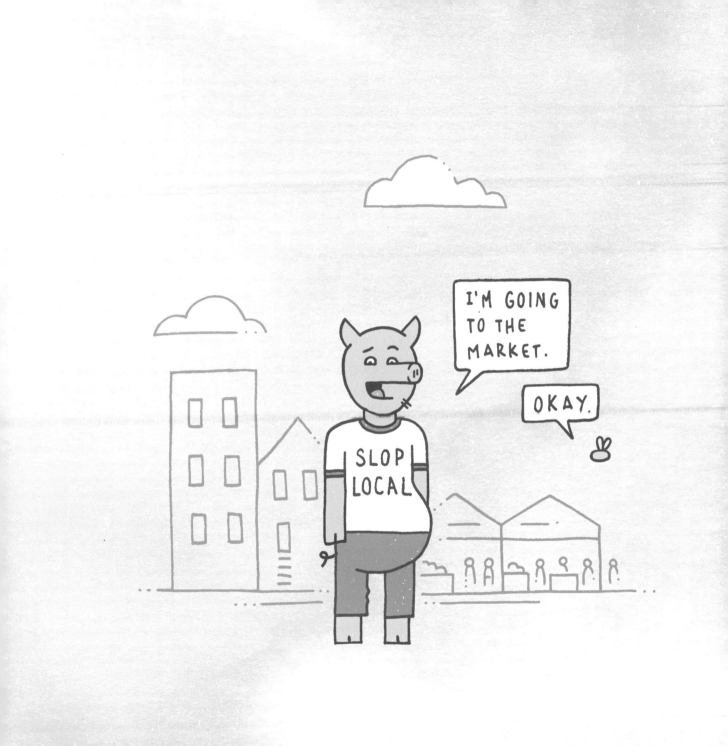

This little piggy

STAYED HOME.

(She always forgets

about the market.)

Z Z Z
X FIT

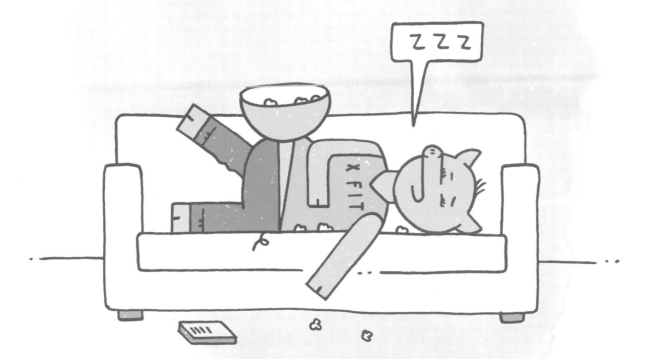

COFFEE

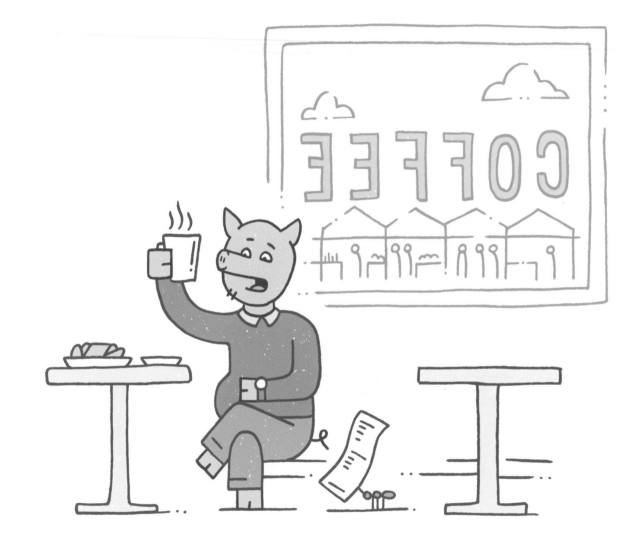

This little piggy made it
all the way to the market, but
when he saw the crowds,
HE JUST COULDN'T EVEN.
So he left and got some
pour-over coffee
and an almond croissant.

This little piggy
will probably end up
**THROWING MOST
OF THIS AWAY.**

EIEIO

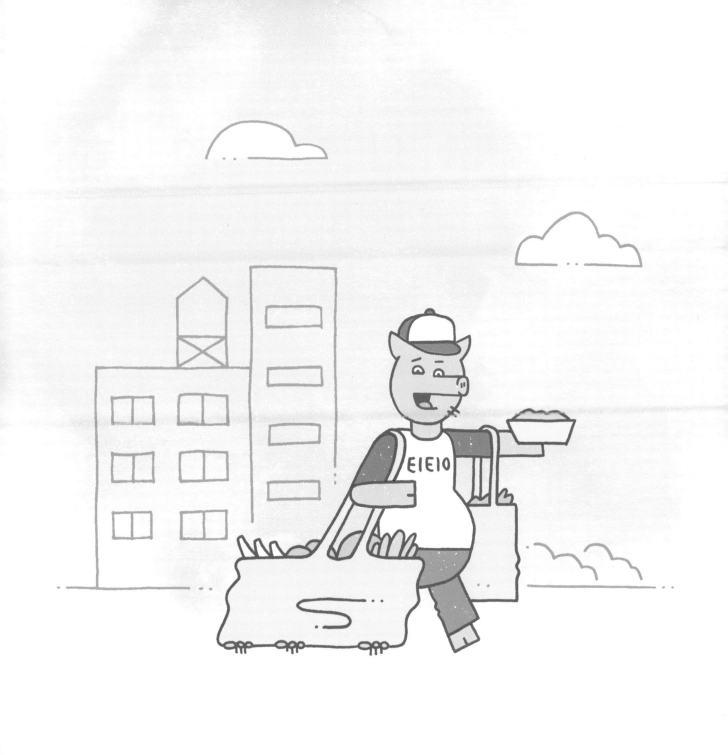

JUHROYEAH?
?
QUICHE?
GROOJÉER?
GROOYEE?
?
GROWYOEY?
FANCY SWISS?
JRÚYEAR?
VREEYOLE?
FRO-YO?
?
GROOWAY?
?

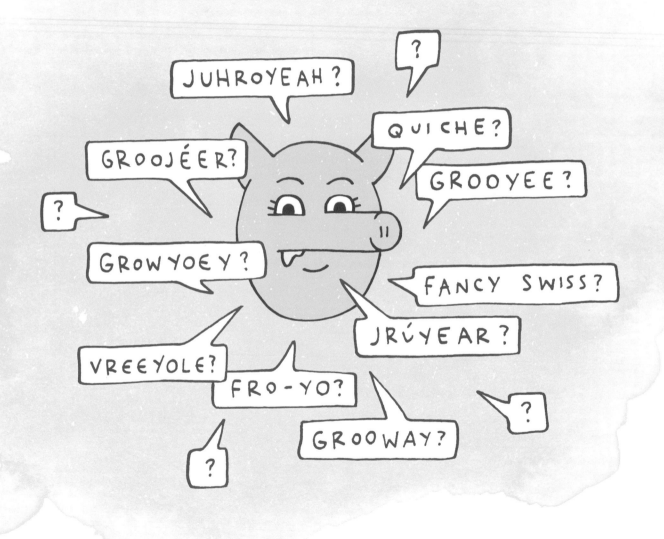

This little piggy wanted some
GRUYÉRE CHEESE but panicked
because she wasn't sure
how to pronounce gruyére
so she got **CHEDDAR** instead.

This little piggy forgot
her tote bag that says

"SATURYAY"

and she is really
BUMMED about it.

This little piggy went to market to canvass for his local **COUNCIL PIG.**

I'M VOTING FOR THE GADFLY CANDIDATE.

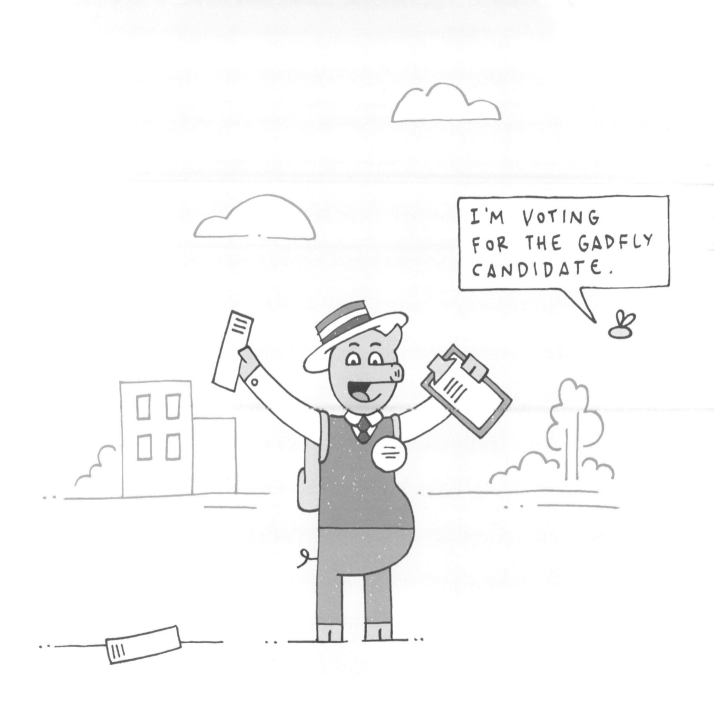

This little piggy is

COMPOSTING.

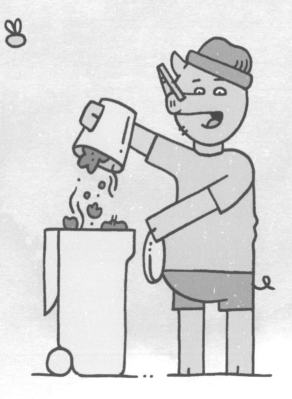

This little piggy is thinking,
"WHAT EXACTLY IS COMPOSTING?"

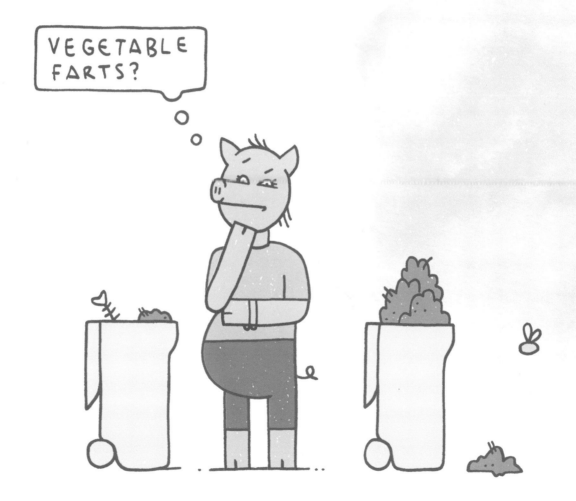

This little piggy got into
a conversation with
THE FISH GUY.
And now I guess
he's **EATING HALIBUT**
for dinner tonight.
And breakfast tomorrow.
And lunch after that.

I WONDER IF I LIKE HALIBUT?

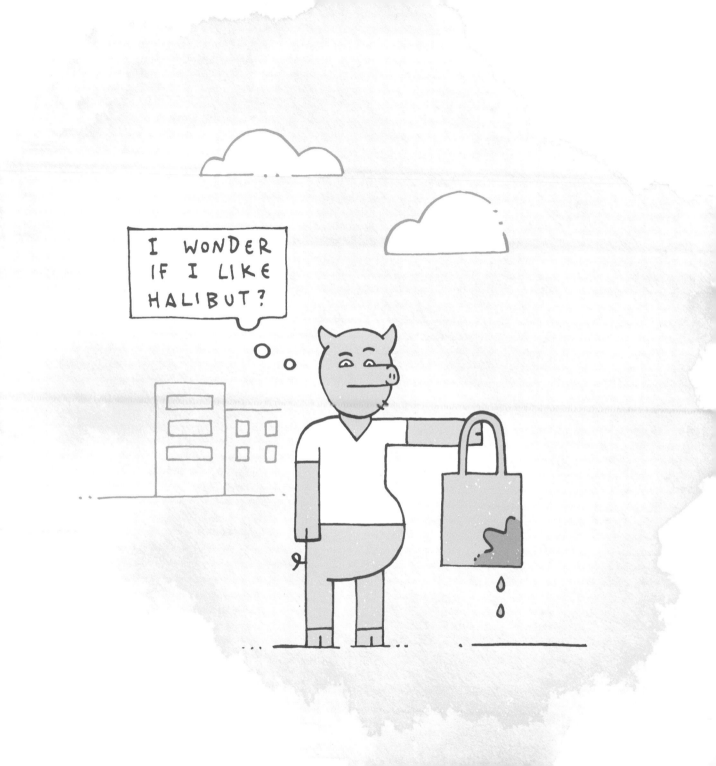

This little piggy had

ROAST BEEF

but is struggling
to pick an artisanal
mustard to go with it.

This little piggy just asked
if the **ROAST BEEF** was
KETO FRIENDLY.
Because this little piggy is
INSUFFERABLE.

This little piggy

had **NONE.**

YES, HONEY!

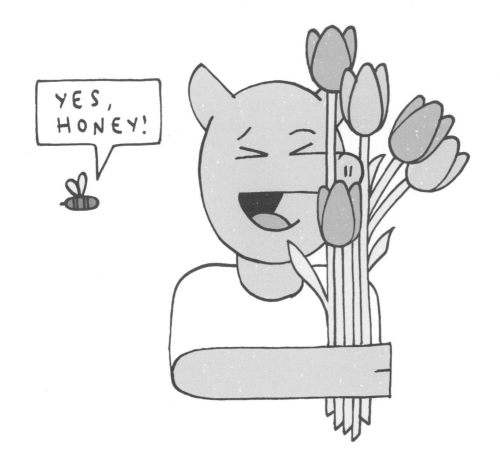

This little piggy is buying
FLOWERS for himself.
Because they are beautiful
and toxic masculinity is
#CANCELLED.

These little piggies went

WEE-WEE-WEE

all the way **HOME.**

HONESTLY, I DON'T EVEN MISS BREAD.

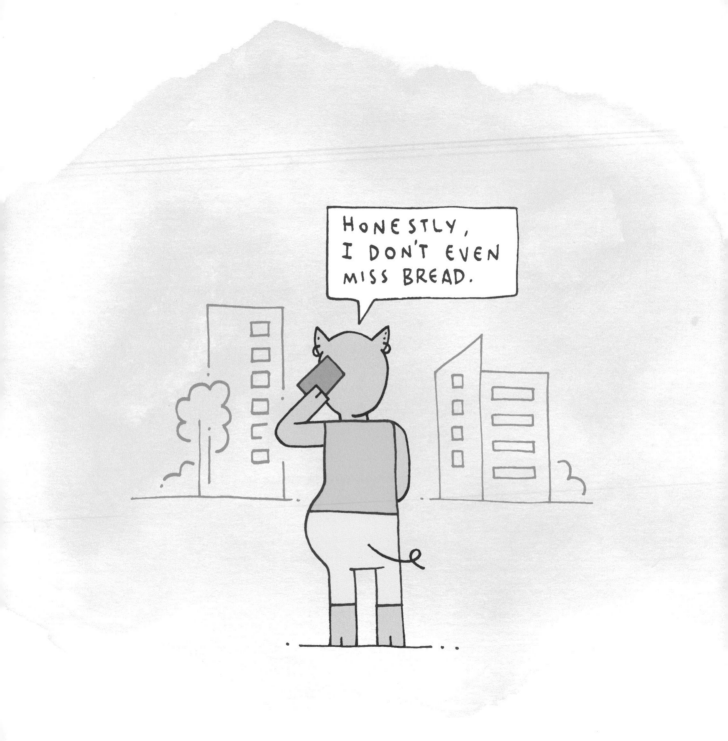

THE END

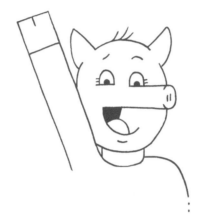

TARA LAWALL is a writer, advertising person, and aspiring "cool mom." She lives in Brooklyn with her husband, Jeremy, and kids, Cora and Rhett. This is her first book. So thank you more than normal for buying it.

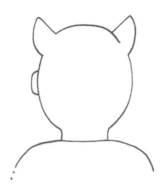

RICH GRECO is a designer and illustrator from Brooklyn, working in the field of advertising. Throughout his career, Rich has stayed grounded. If he could fly, he wouldn't. He loves the ground. He really digs ditches, as well as wells.

Skyhorse Publishing books may be purchased in bulk at special discounts for
sales promotion, corporate gifts, fund-raising, or educational purposes. Special
editions can also be created to specifications. For details, contact the Special
Sales Department, Skyhorse Publishing, 307 West 36th Street, 11th Floor,
New York, NY 10018 or info@skyhorsepublishing.com.

Skyhorse® and Skyhorse Publishing® are registered trademarks of Skyhorse
Publishing, Inc.®, a Delaware corporation.

Visit our website at www.skyhorsepublishing.com.

10 9 8 7 6 5 4 3 2 1

Library of Congress Cataloging-in-Publication Data is available on file.

Cover design and illustration by Rich Greco

Print ISBN: 978-1-5107-6276-3
Ebook ISBN: 978-1-5107-6277-0

Printed in China